150 WAYS TO TELL IF YOU'RE GHETTO

BY SHAWN WAYANS, CHRIS SPENCER, & SULI MCCULLOUGH

ILLUSTRATIONS BY GEORGE HAY

A Dell Trade Paperback

A DELL TRADE PAPERBACK

Published by
Dell Publishing
a division of
Bantam Doubleday Dell Publishing Group, Inc.
1540 Broadway, New York, New York 10036

Library of Congress Cataloging in Publication Data

Wayans, Shawn, 1971–
　　　　　　　　　[150 ways to know if you're ghetto]
　　　　　　　　　150 ways to tell if you're ghetto / Shawn Wayans, Chris Spencer,
　　　　　　　　　and Suli McCullough.
　　　　　　　　　　　　　p.　　　cm.
　　　　　　　　　ISBN 0-440-50793-6
　　　　　　　　　1. Inner cities—United States—Humor.　2. Afro-American wit and humor.
　　　　　　　3. Afro-Americans—Social life and customs—Humor.
　　　　　　　I. Spencer, Chris, 1968–　　.　II. McCullough, Suli, 1968–　　.　III. Title.
　　　　　　　[PN6231.I54W38　1997]
　　　　　　　818'.5402—dc21
　　　　　　　　　　　　　　　　　　　　　　96-54857
　　　　　　　　　　　　　　　　　　　　　　CIP

Cover and book design by Michael Grant

Printed in the United States of America

Published simultaneously in Canada

July 1997

10 9 8 7

FFG

O.K. **So you're probably asking yourself why we three decided to write this book....**

Well, back in 1992, we started shooting *Don't Be a Menace to South Central While Drinking Your Juice in the Hood.* Making a movie can be a slow process, so we started entertaining ourselves when we weren't filming by throwing out these ghetto one-liners. After days of serious laughter, we realized this was something we just couldn't keep to ourselves, so we decided to write a book.

But what does it mean to be ghetto? Well, on one level, ghetto is just ghetto, and if you have to **ax,** you'll never know. To offer a more scientific explanation, being "ghetto" is doing those little things we all do that, when you stop to think about it, can ultimately be traced back to the ghetto. But don't misunderstand. Ghetto is **more than just a place.** It has little to do with what color you are, where you live, or how much money you have. **Anybody** can be ghetto. You can live in Beverly Hills and be ghetto. If Hillary Clinton ever picked Chelsea up from school with rollers in her hair ... Guess what? The First Lady be **ghetto.**

GHETTO SYMPTOMS
- COLOR-COORDINATED BEEPER
- CAP & SNEAKERS HAVE BRAND TAGS
- INDIGESTION FROM FRIED BALONEY SANDWICH
- WAY TOO MUCH GOLD

We hope this book brings you as many laughs as it did for us. Many of the things in here we've done ourselves or know someone who's done them. So we're not (really) trying to offend anybody. But if you do get offended, chances are it's because...

YOU'RE GHETTO!   — Shawn, Chris, & Suli

YOU KNOW YOU'RE
GHETTO
IF...

You can make a Hyundai go 120 mph.

❖

Your kids are in your wedding.

❖

You put sugar on your frosted cornflakes.

❖

The police know your entire family.

You got married in prison.

YOU KNOW YOU'RE GHETTO IF...

You use your hands to put food on your fork.

❖

You call your mom by her first name. "Did you cook, Pearl?"

❖

You're still proud of your Jheri curl.

❖

You own a copy of the Jayne and Leon Isaac Kennedy video.

You iron dirty clothes.

YOU KNOW YOU'RE

GHETTO

IF...

**The only vegetable in your diet
is the lettuce from a Big Mac.**

❖

You pop your gum at a job interview.

❖

You've ever been a guest on *Ricki Lake*.

❖

Karl Kani made your wedding dress.

You wear house shoes to the grocery store.

You're nineteen and you just met your father.

You've ever slapped someone over the prize in the cereal box.

You use a clothes hanger as a TV antenna.

YOU KNOW YOU'RE

GHETTO
IF...

**You have a wife and kids but
still live with your parents.**

❖

You don't have two pieces of ID.

❖

You didn't know there were two Lionels on *The Jeffersons*.

❖

You chew ice.

❖

You ~~caint~~ ~~kant~~ can't spell "can't."

You recognize your homies on *America's Most Wanted*.

You work out at a jungle gym.

YOU KNOW YOU'RE GHETTO IF...

You record over previously recorded tapes.

**You were happy when they tore down
the library to build another liquor store.**

You steal and get beat only for getting caught.

You still wear anything that says "Whoop, there it is."

You've ever worn a doo rag to court.

Your mom does your hair in the kitchen.

YOU KNOW YOU'RE
GHETTO
IF...

You go to school just to sell drugs.

❖

You don't pay your rent until you're served with a three-day notice.

❖

You pick your shaving bumps in public.

❖

You put on panty hose instead of shaving your legs.

You got all new appliances the day after the riots.

You're getting paid, but your bills ain't.

YOU KNOW YOU'RE

GHETTO
IF...

Your moms washes paper plates.

❖

**You buy clothes for a party and
return them to the store the next day.**

❖

You only go to church on Easter and Mother's Day.

❖

You drink a soda with breakfast.

You throw a pool party at the fire hydrant.

YOU KNOW YOU'RE GHETTO IF...

You think Tupac faked his death.

❖

You use your oven to dry wet clothes.

❖

Your first name begins with Ta', La', or Sha'.

❖

The windows in your house have
more cardboard than glass.

You took the batteries out of the smoke detector to put in your pager.

YOU KNOW YOU'RE GHETTO IF...

Your bank is a check-cashing place.

❖

**The Santa Claus at your mall
doesn't have the red and white outfit.**

❖

You still put your Members Only jacket in the cleaners.

❖

You buy pagers to match your outfits.

You have graffiti on your shower curtains.

Your teacher is afraid to teach you.

YOU KNOW YOU'RE GHETTO IF...

You were close enough to hit Reginald Denny.

❖

You go trick-or-treating without a costume.

❖

You pee in the shower.

❖

You have to put stuff on layaway
at the 99-cent store.

You play tackle football on concrete.

YOU KNOW YOU'RE

GHETTO

IF...

You brush your teeth with a washcloth.

❖

Your man can wear his hair in a ponytail but you can't.

❖

You buy cigarettes individually, not by the pack.

❖

You ask your wife for money to pay for your girlfriend's abortion.

❖

You do your grocery shopping at the liquor store.

You jump into a fight that doesn't involve you.

YOU KNOW YOU'RE GHETTO IF...

You can hear your heater but you can't feel it.

❖

You have a drawer full of catsup, jelly, salt,
and napkins from fast-food restaurants.

❖

You think you should be the *Jet* beauty of the week.

❖

You wrap Christmas presents in newspaper.

You walk your pit bull without a leash.

You're uncomfortable about living somewhere that **<u>doesn't</u>** have roaches.

YOU KNOW YOU'RE
GHETTO
IF...

Your landlord is afraid to come to your apartment.

❖

You think Al Sharpton should be President.

❖

You slept with your babysitter.

❖

You're hooked on ebonics.

❖

**You think putting batteries in
the refrigerator recharges them.**

You have a lock on your phone.

You can outrun a police dog.

YOU KNOW YOU'RE
GHETTO
IF...

**When you were little you had to be
in the house before the streetlights came on.**

❖

You think you can kick Mike Tyson's ass.

❖

You go to church just to pick up women.

❖

You've ever had to have a police escort to a baby shower.

There's a black Jesus in your living room.

You take a bubble bath with dishwashing liquid.

YOU KNOW YOU'RE GHETTO IF...

You write down your phone number
with eyeliner or lipstick.

❖

You found your dog.

❖

Your boxers are longer than your shorts.

❖

You return gifts for the money.

**It was okay
to have D's
on your
report card.**

REPORT CARD
ENGLISH - D
MATHS - D
RECESS - D

You get into a fistfight while you're pregnant.

YOU KNOW YOU'RE

IF...

You still think Billy Dee Williams is fine.

❖

You have more than one social security number.

❖

You yell "Pookie" in your house and five people turn around.

❖

You used to play Hide and Go Get It.

You think going to prison is "keeping it real."

You missed the birth of your child because you were playing Sega.

Your mom can pop a wheelie on a ten-speed.

YOU KNOW YOU'RE
GHETTO
IF...

You save cooking grease.

❖

**You left Las Vegas mad because
they didn't have a domino table.**

❖

**Your woman has more hair on her legs
than you have on your chest.**

❖

Your uncle still has furry dice hanging from his rearview mirror.

You've ever gone to a nightclub with the flu.

YOU KNOW YOU'RE
GHETTO
IF...

There's a metal detector at your kid's day care.

❖

You use one tea bag for six cups of tea.

❖

You defend weaves.

❖

The only dates marked on your calendar are
the first and the fifteenth.

You dropped out of high school to become a Def Jam comic.

Your DKNY sweatshirt has an extra letter.

YOU KNOW YOU'RE
GHETTO
IF...

You think Rodney King is sexy.

❖

**You can't go outside until your brother
comes home with the jacket.**

❖

You bought your Christmas tree the day after Christmas.

❖

Your mom whups your friends.

The star on your Christmas tree is a Mercedes-Benz emblem.

YOU KNOW YOU'RE
GHETTO
IF...

You keep food stamps in a money clip.

YOU KNOW YOU'RE
GHETTO
IF...

You think grease and water make your hair curly.

❖

You wear tube socks with dress shoes.

❖

**You know who Divine Brown is,
but don't know who Hugh Grant is.**

❖

You're still doing the running man.

You Know You're GHETTO If...

You have the phone numbers to several prisons on speed dial.

You fight over the banana with the sticker on it.

YOU KNOW YOU'RE

GHETTO

IF...

**You call celebrities by their character's name:
"Hey, Moesha!" "What's up, Urkel."**

❖

You add water to shampoo to stretch it.

❖

You put your kids to sleep with NyQuil.

❖

You use your welfare check as collateral.

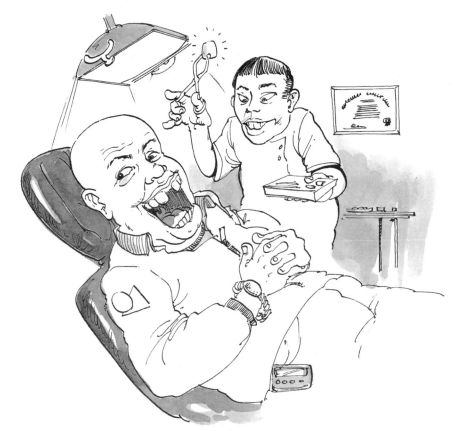

You have a gold cap over a cavity.

YOU KNOW YOU'RE
GHETTO
IF...

You primed your car and never
got around to painting over it.

❖

You use a toothbrush to style your baby hair.

❖

You thought *Good Times* was a documentary.

❖

The soap in your bathroom is the size of a Tic-Tac
and you're still trying to use it.

You named your daughters after cars you can't afford.

You can outrun a cop while wearing high heels.

YOU KNOW YOU'RE
GHETTO
IF...

You bought your rims before you bought your car.

❖

You have the Spam key on your key ring.

❖

You think going on a diet means no candy.

❖

You use your brother as a blanket.

Your fingernails are longer than your fingers.

You've ever tried to drive your car with the boot on it.

You think jury duty is a good way to make money.

You got beat with those orange plastic race car tracks.

YOU KNOW YOU'RE

GHETTO

IF...

You thought killing somebody would get you
a deal with Death Row Records.

❖

You think boxing is your only way out of the hood.

❖

You use the light from your TV to do your homework.

❖

You bought your Benz with cash.

❖

You owned a copy of this book before it came out.

DEDICATION AND ACKNOWLEDGMENTS

Shawn Wayans

I'd like to dedicate this book to my mother and father, Elvira and Howell Wayans, who sacrificed so much of their own lives and dreams to raise me and my brothers and sisters the way that they did. I know times got hard but I appreciate the two of you hanging in there and keeping a stable, warm, loving environment for me and my siblings. I love you with all my heart.

I'd like to thank God for blessing me with my wonderful family and also the talent to do what we do.

Thanks to my brother Keenen for making my childhood the best childhood any little project boy could have. Your time, patience, and guidance have made me the man I am today. You taught me everything I know. You are truly a great man and the best Big Brother in the world. You gets mad props Ivory. I love you.

Special thanks to my nigga Damonson. Thanks for teaching me the ins and outs of stand-up comedy. Just watching you inspires me. You're the best. You are also one of the best Big Brothers anyone could ask for. I love you.

Special thanks to my sister Kim for always being there for me no matter what. You're not just the greatest Big Sister but you're one of my best friends. I love you.

Special thanks to my nigga Naz. You are my little egg. I so glad mama made me a little brother like you. You're my heart. Me and you, baby. Much love.

To the rest of the Way-tang Clan—Elvira, Deidra, Nadia, Vonnie, Dwayne C-Low, D-Rock, Shiky Chunt'e, Summer, etc . . . much love, you're all in my heart.

Special thanks to Ooshi for all of your love and support. You are a strong woman. I love you.

Special thanks to my manager Eric Larry Gold and the Gold/Miller Co. Thanks for all of your hard work and belief in me. You're the best, hardest working manager in the business. I love you.

Special thanks to Jim Stein and Norman Aladjem for keeping this project going and all your hard work.

Special thanks to "Daper Dan" for all of your love and support throughout the years. Like you said, "It's all good." I ain't mad atchya—one love.

To all of my friends—Twist, White Phil, Buddy love, Devon, Fire Fly-Danny guru-Chris Rock, Chris Spencer, Suli, Darryl, Alex, Dwayne, Mary-Tess, One love.

To J.P. and Debbie Williams. Thanks for all your hard work and loyalty throughout the years. I love you guys.

Special thanks to Jamie Masada and the Laugh Factory. Clean Comedy Buddy.

And last but not least, a very special thanks to my loving granny. Thanks for all your love and support. Thanks for paying that Korean grocer back when I stole those gingersnaps when I was a little child. Love you, child.

Chris Spencer

First and foremost, I would like to give special thanks to all those who created my funny. My mom, Dorothy Panton, my stepfather, Adrian Panton, my father Carlton Spencer, where all of my wit derived from, and my sisters Kim Spencer and Nadra Panton. I would also like to thank those who helped me nurture this insane sense of humor I have: Sid Cooke, Robert Parada, Devon Smith, Xavier Cook, Xavier Mora, Sharif Salaway, Chris Bodaken, Rueben Paul, Tony Fleming, Sean Hackley, Lauris Freeman, Robert Walker, the Elliot family, everyone at Balboa gym and the Hollywood YMCA, Prophet Jennings, who told me to explore the edge, my two partners in crime (and not just comedy), Darrel Heath and Alex Thomas, Duane and Tisha Martin, Will and Jada, Kisha Maldonado, Bruce Fine for giving me my first pornography tape, Tommy Morgan, Burt Harris, the entire Wayans organization (all 160), Ross Mark of the Improv, Jamie Masada of the Laugh Factory (who gave me my start?), Larry Easterwood for reasons only I know, John Caldwell, Brooklyn McLynn, Damen Dozier, Donyell Kennedy, Julissa Marquez, Edwin Marcellin, my grandmother—Gwendolyn Pitter—who is probably the funniest of them all but doesn't realize it, Auntie Ditty, Stan and Lois Pitter-Bruce, Budd Friedman, Michelle Herndon, Quincy Jones, David Salzman, Keith Clinkscales, everyone at Columbia Tri-Star, the "Vibe" show staff, everyone at QDe, and everyone at Qwest Records. A super special thanks to my beautiful management team of J.P. Williams, Debbie Shaler, and Maggie Houlehan for believing in me and my debts. I would also like to extend a special thanks to Jeff Foxworthy for inspiration and words of wisdom. Last but not least, I attribute my bitter edge to all of those who have dissed me. Thanks, y'all.

Suli McCullough

I wish to thank everyone that helped to make this book a reality. A very special thanks to my mom, Betty Moore; without you none of this would be possible. To my brothers and sisters Shahid, Shaman, Sharob, Sayyeda, Davia, and David. Thanks to all my family out there, uncles, aunts, and cousins. To Donyell Kennedy, thanks for all your love and support. Many thanks also go out to all my friends: Lauris Freeman, Alex Thomas and TaDarrel Heath, Steve and Annabeth White, Bruce Fine, Jeff Cesario, Keenen Wayans, Damon Wayans, Marlon Wayans, Kim Wayans, Chris Rock, Sean Hackley, Mitch Mullany, Mark Curry, George and Ann Lopez, Leslie and Steven Perry, Bill and Therese White, Dominique and Prophet Jennings, Dwayne and Tisha, Jamie and Marcus King, Jeb, Joko and Kebe Dunn. To Tony Edwards and Angelique, thank you for the jokes. We appreciate the time and effort. On the business side, thanks to my managers Diane Barnett, George Shapiro, Howard West, Scott Gertz, and everyone else in the office. Thanks to Eric Gold, Jamie Masada, Budd Friedman, and Mark Lonow. I'd like to thank Cherise Davis Grant at Dell for putting up with us. I'm gonna miss calling you while you're out at lunch. To SW1 and Chris "Hollywood" Spencer, thanks for the hard work and . . . "JOKES"! Let's continue to not be docile. Finally, if there's anyone I forgot, I'm sorry, but we had a deadline!